Contents

Is something lurking in this house?

A house is a place where you eat, sleep, work, and play. The bathroom is where you can go to get clean or use the toilet. But do you know what might be living in your bathroom?

In This Bathroom

Nancy Harris

www.raintreepublishers.co.uk
Visit our website to find out
more information about
Raintree books.

To order:
☎ Phone 0845 6044371
🖨 Fax +44 (0) 1865 312263
📧 Email myorders@raintreepublishers.co.uk

Customers from outside the UK please telephone +44 1865 312262

Raintree is an imprint of Capstone Global Library Limited,
a company incorporated in England and Wales having its
registered office at 7 Pilgrim Street, London, EC4V 6LB
– Registered company number: 6695582

Text © Capstone Global Library Limited 2010
First published in hardback in 2010
First published in paperback in 2011
The moral rights of the proprietor have been asserted.

Edited by Rebecca Rissman, Nancy Dickmann,
and Sian Smith
Designed by Joanna Hinton-Malivoire
Original illustrations © Capstone Global Library Ltd., 2010
Illustrated by Kevin Rechin
Picture research by Tracy Cummins
Originated by Capstone Global Library Ltd
Printed and bound in China by Leo Paper
Products Ltd

ISBN 978 140621317 1 (hardback)
14 13 12 11 10
10 9 8 7 6 5 4 3 2 1

ISBN 978 140621323 2 (paperback)
14 13 12 11 10
10 9 8 7 6 5 4 3 2 1

British Library Cataloguing in Publication Data
Harris, Nancy.
  What's lurking in this house?.
  In this bathroom.
  1. Household pests--Juvenile literature. 2. Microbial
  ecology--Juvenile literature. 3. Bathrooms--Juvenile
  literature.
  I. Title
  579.1'7-dc22

Acknowledgements
The author and publisher are grateful to the following for
permission to reproduce copyright material: Alamy pp.**18**
(© Richard Ryland); Getty Images pp.**26 bottom** (Frank
Greenaway), **28** (Barry Austin Photography); istockphoto
pp.**8** (Oleg Prikhodko), **16** (Clayton Cole), **17** (© Shaun
Lowe), **26 top** (© James Richey); Photo Researchers, Inc.
pp.**9**, **13** (© Scimat), **14** (© Steve Gschmeissner), **11** (©
Dr. Jeremy Burgess), **21** (© Edward Lettau), **23** (© Scott
Camazine), **25** (© Eye of Science); Photolibrary pp.**10**
(A Chederros), **12** (Sean Justice); Shutterstock p.**15** (©
stocksnapp); Visuals Unlimited, Inc. p.**7** (© Dr. Dennis
Kunke).
Cover photograph of a house centipede reproduced with
permission of Alamy (© Todd Bannor).

Every effort has been made to contact copyright holders
of any material reproduced in this book. Any omissions
will be rectified in subsequent printings if notice is given
to the publisher.

Some words are shown in bold, **like this**. You can find
out what they mean by looking in the glossary.

How clean are you?

You go into the bathroom and turn on the bath taps. You get in the bath and wash. You get out and feel squeaky clean. But how can you be clean if your bathroom is full of living things called **germs**?

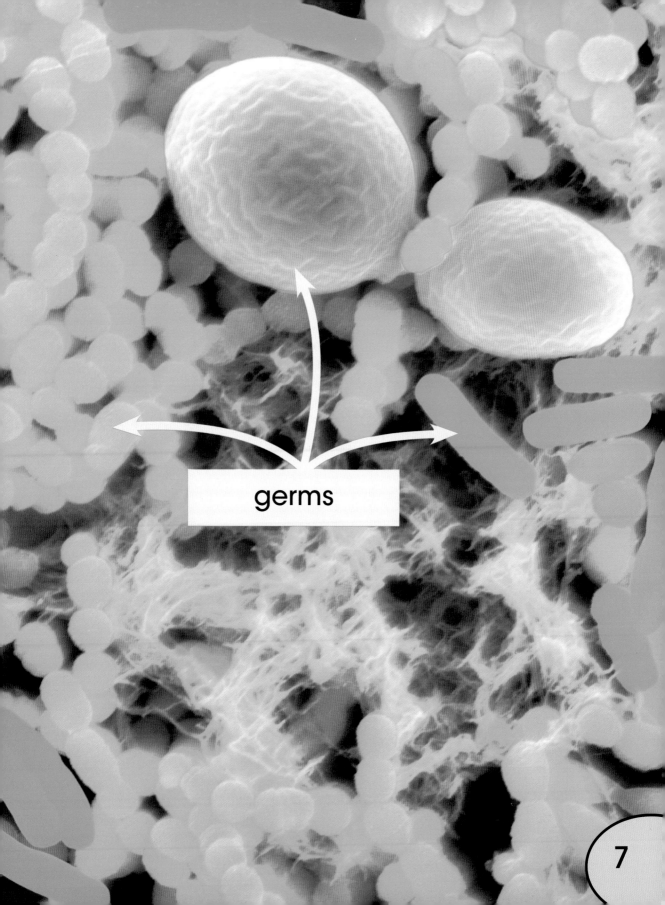

germs

Dangerous germs

Germs are very small living things. You need to look at them through a **microscope** to see them. There are many types of germs. Germs can make you ill.

FUN FACT

Germs don't just live on the things in your bathroom. They can live on you too!

microscope

Don't let the pretty colours of these germs fool you. They can cause some nasty illnesses.

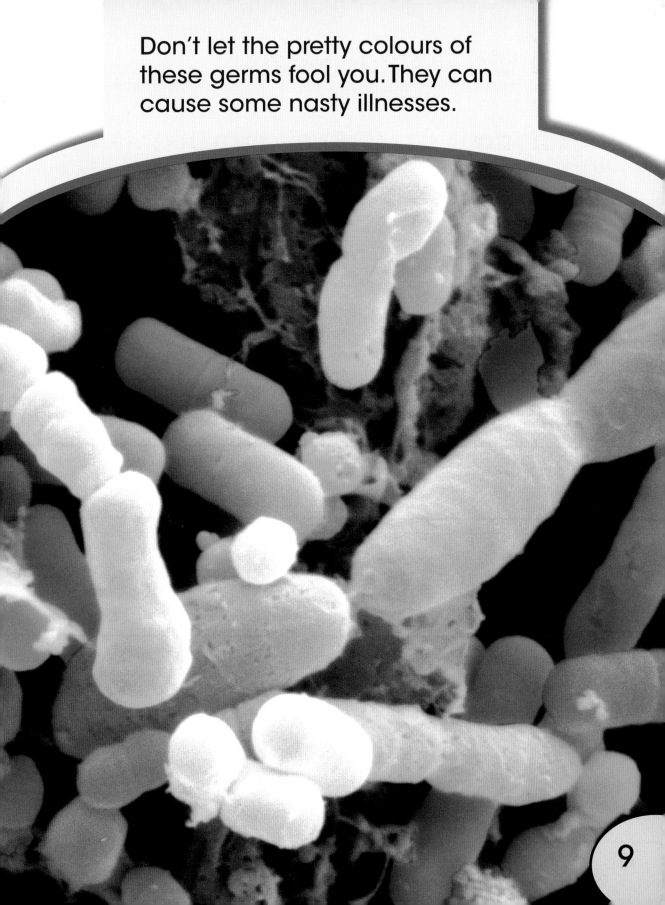

Snacking on skin

Bacteria are a type of **germ**. Bacteria eat the dead parts of plants and animals. Little bits of dead skin drop off us every day. Bacteria like to eat the dead skin pieces.

More dead skin comes off when you rub yourself dry with a towel. This gives bacteria plenty to munch on.

Dead skin seen through a microscope.

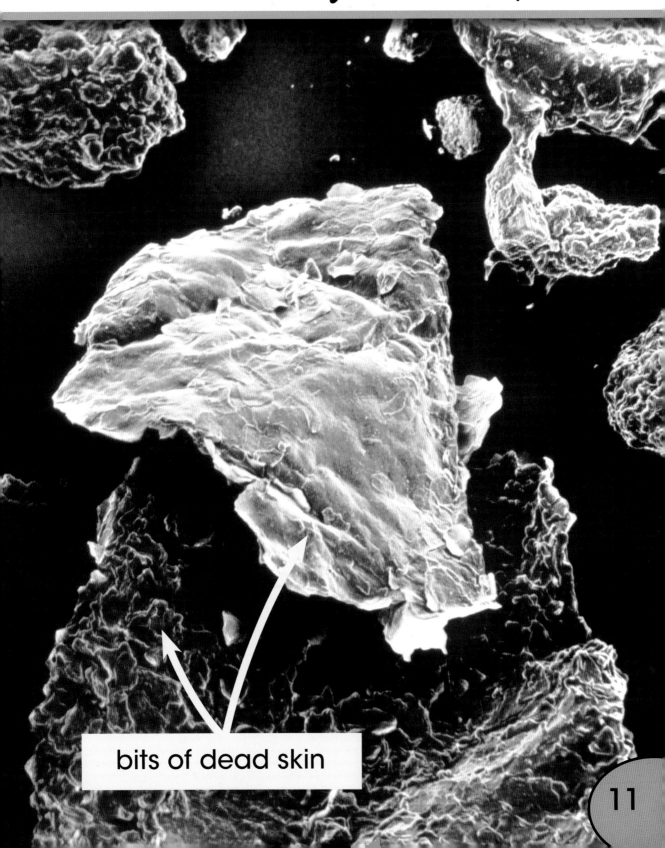

bits of dead skin

Getting ill

Bacteria grow in your toilet bowl and on the toilet handle. They can fly out of your toilet as the dirty water is being flushed down.

Always wash your hands after you have been to the toilet. This stops **germs** from getting into your body and making you ill.

Poo is full of dangerous bacteria that can make you very ill. This is what bacteria on poo looks like under a **microscope**.

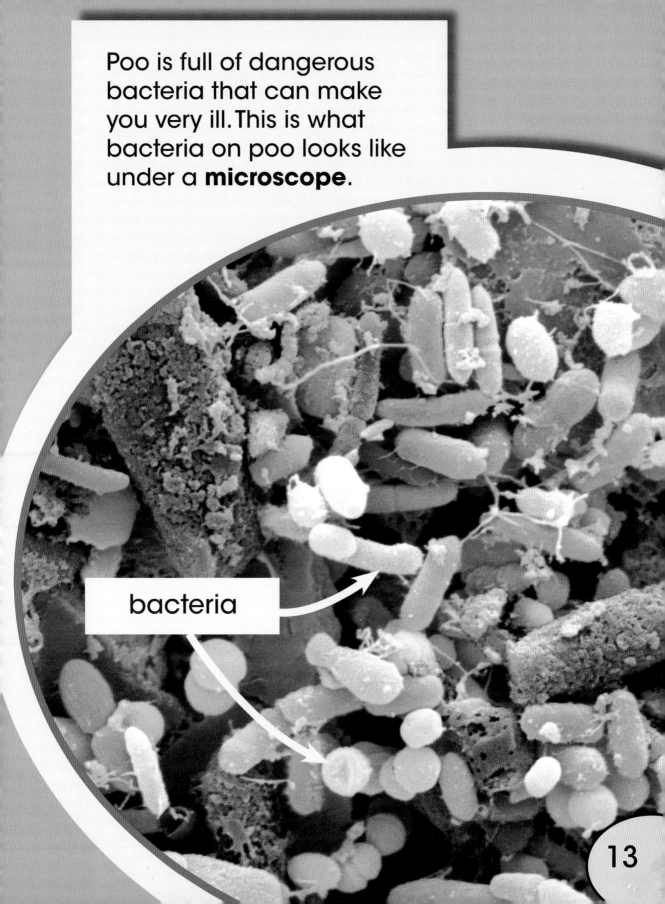

bacteria

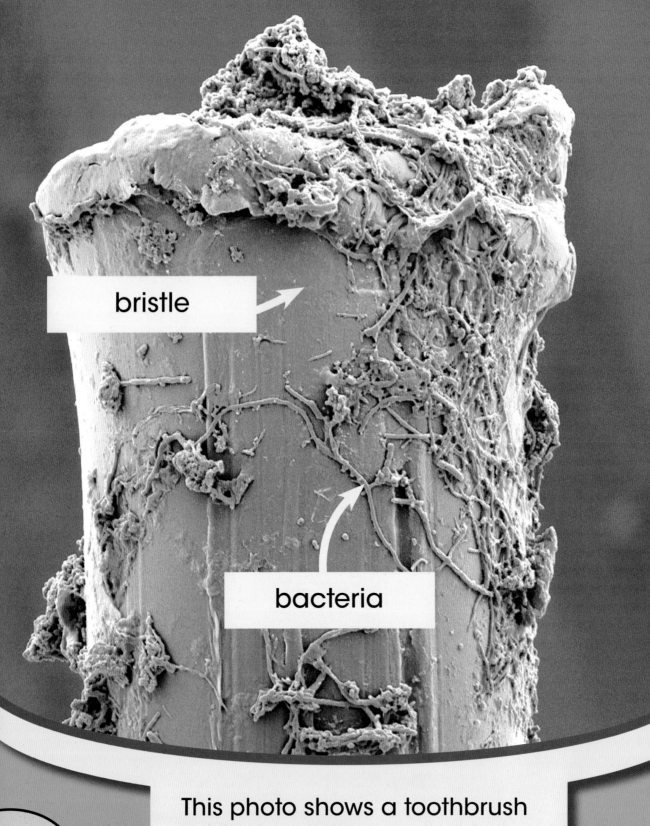

bristle

bacteria

This photo shows a toothbrush bristle up close.

Bacteria also grow on your toothbrush! Bacteria can give you sore gums. The good news is that you can easily stop this happening. Get a new toothbrush every three months!

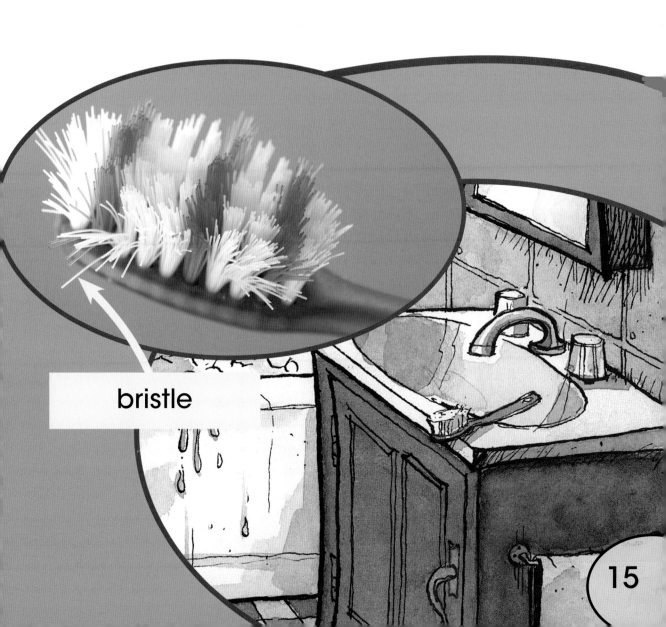

bristle

Masses of mould

Mould is a small living thing. Mould likes to live in warm, wet places. It is easy to see why mould likes to live in the bathroom!

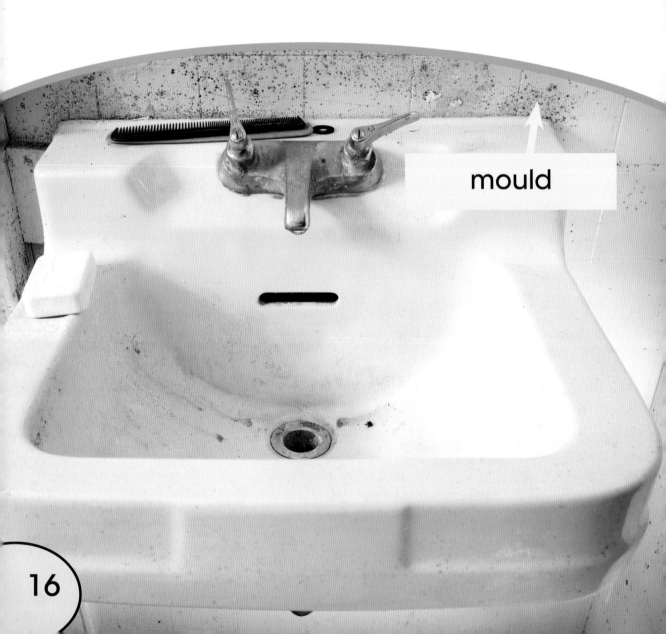

mould

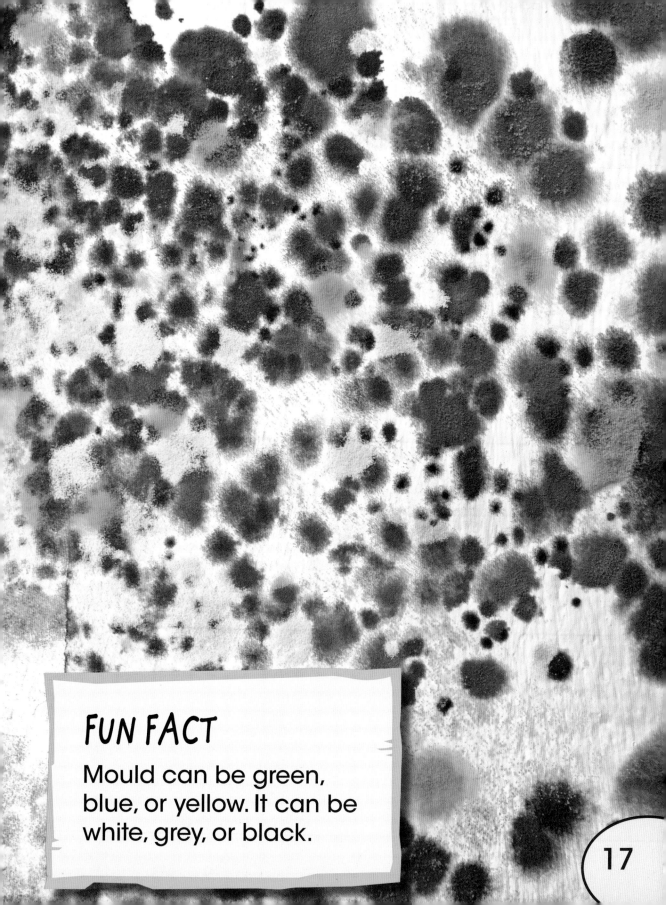

FUN FACT

Mould can be green, blue, or yellow. It can be white, grey, or black.

Would you go in a shower full of black mould?

mould

Mould can grow in many places. It grows on floors and wallpaper. It grows on tiles and carpets. It can grow behind your shower wall and all over your shower curtain.

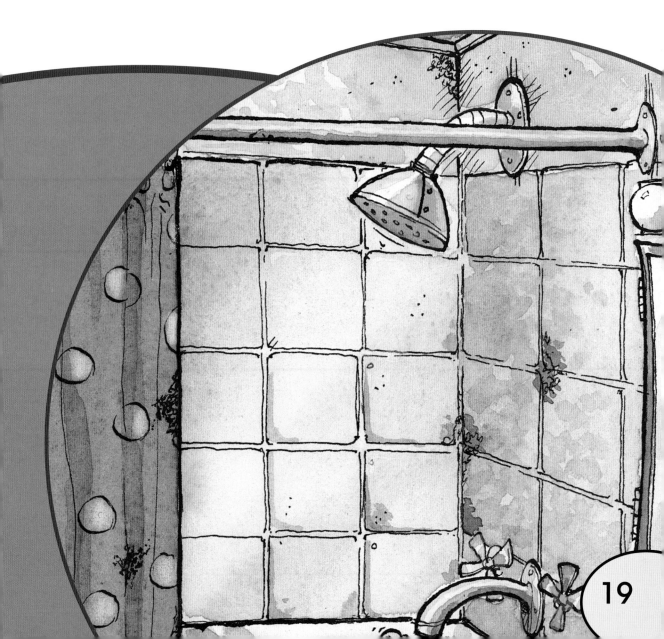

Is mould harmful?

Mould can make you ill. Some people are **allergic** to mould. It makes them sneeze and cough. It can make it hard for them to breathe.

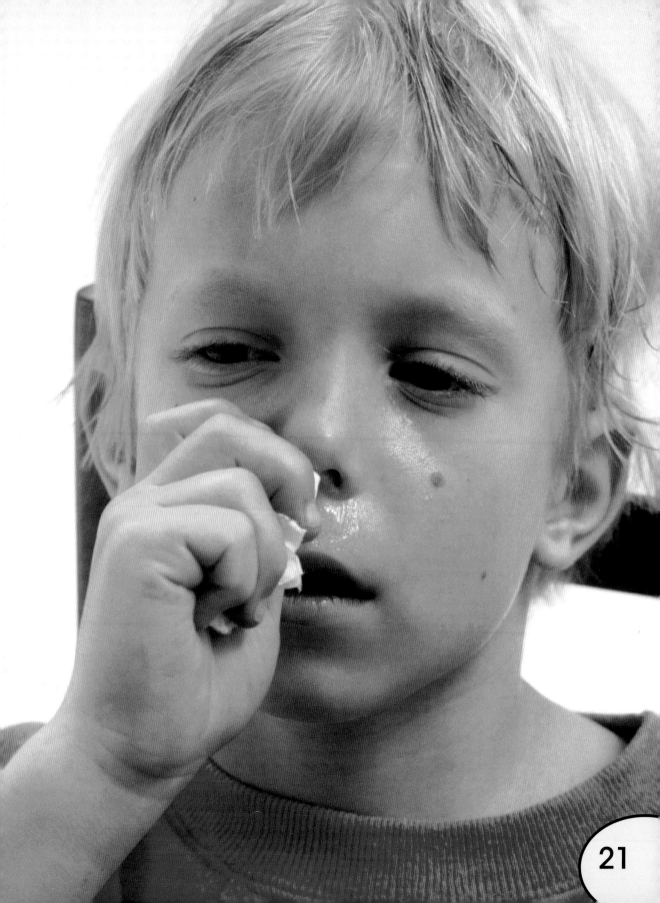

Creepy-crawly creatures

Many types of creatures can lurk in your bathroom. House centipedes may live in the bathroom. They eat insects. They usually eat at night while you are sleeping.

FUN FACT

House centipedes have 15 pairs of legs. Imagine how fast they can move!

centipede

legs

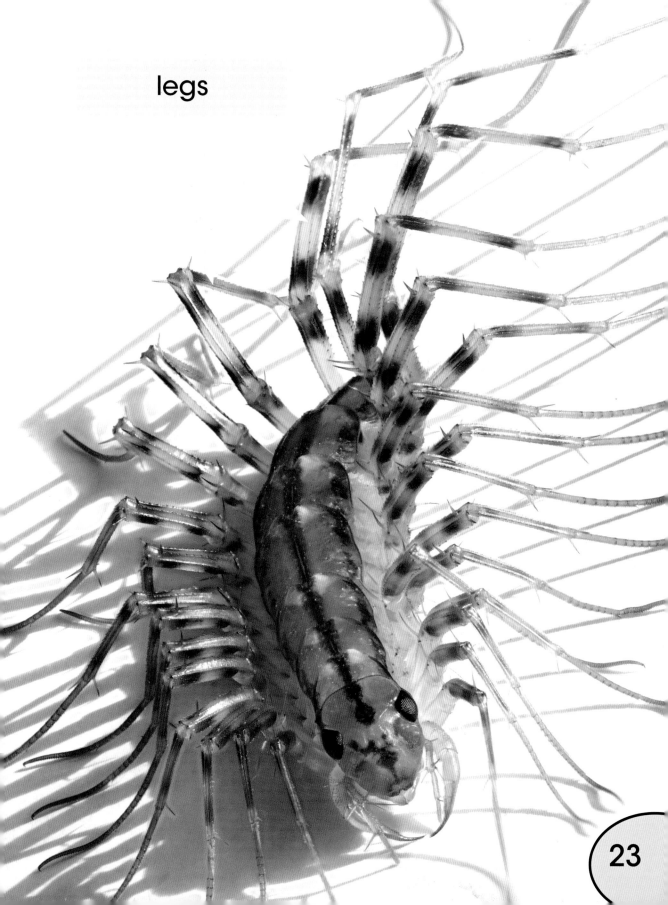

Silverfish are insects that may live in your bathroom. They are silver or brown in colour. They are **nocturnal**. Silverfish come out at night to eat.

FUN FACT

Silverfish eat wallpaper, glue, and mould.

silverfish

Adult silverfish are about a centimetre long. That's about the same length as a sunflower seed.

This photo shows a silverfish up close.

House centipedes will sometimes bite people. Silverfish do not. Which creature would you rather find lurking in your bathroom?

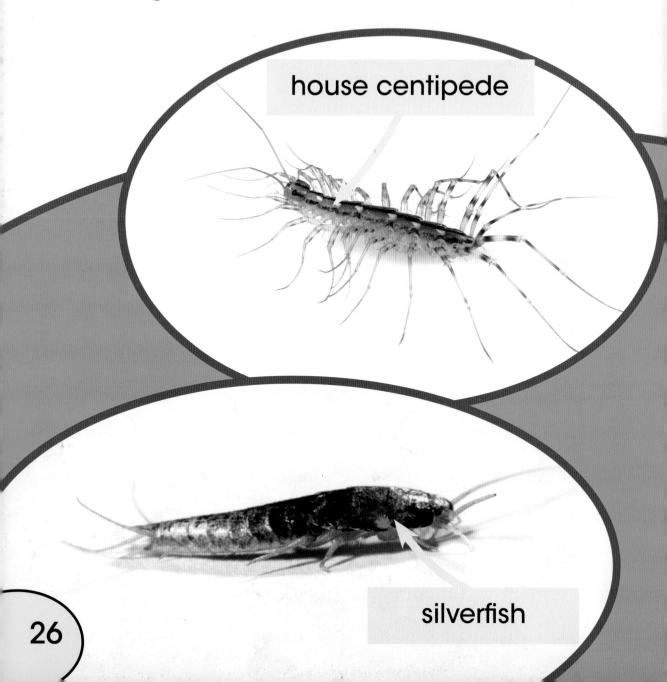

house centipede

silverfish

FUN FACT

House centipedes will eat silverfish and other pests.

27

Keeping it clean

It is important to keep the bathroom clean. Use a special cleaner that kills **germs**. This will help to control the **bacteria**, mould, and creatures in the bathroom.

Fun facts

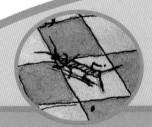

Silverfish can survive for a year or more without food.

Wash your hands for the same length of time as it takes to say the alphabet. This will get them properly clean.

"Centipede" means "one hundred feet". House centipedes only have 15 pairs of feet. Some other types of centipede have more than 100 feet!

If one of a house centipede's legs is held down, the centipede can drop that leg off. The centipede can then escape while its attacker is busy looking at the twitching leg!

Glossary

allergic when you are allergic to something your body reacts badly to it. For example, some people are allergic to mould; it makes them sneeze.

bacteria tiny living things. Bacteria are a type of germ.

germs tiny living things that can make you ill if they get inside your body

microscope instrument used to see very small things, such as germs

nocturnal describes animals that sleep during the daytime and come out at night

Find out more

Books

Checkerboard Science Library: Bugs!: Centipedes, Kristin Petrie (Abdo Publishing, 2008)

Germs, Ross Collins (Bloomsbury Publishing, 2005)

History Horrors: Sick!: Feverish Facts about Blood, Bile and Bacteria, Jim Hatfield (Franklin Watts, 2005)

Where to Find Minibeasts: Minibeasts in the Home, Sarah Ridley (Smart Apple Media, 2009)

Websites

http://kidshealth.org/kid/talk/qa/germs.html
Learn about germs and how to protect yourself from them on this website.

http://www.animalcorner.co.uk/insects/centipedes/centipede_house.html
Use this website to find out about house centipede bites and learn what house centipedes like to eat.

http://www.orkin.com/other/silverfish
Learn about silverfish, house centipedes, and other insects on this website.

Find out

Which bathroom insects sometimes eat shampoo?

Index